MW01173103

BE FIERCE

The Athlete's Guide to Growing Physically, Mentally, and Spiritually

Samantha Kelley

DEDICATION

For Nora.

May you rest in the Peace of Christ.

CONTENTS

ACKNOWLEDGMENTS

Thank you to all who helped make this book possible. Thank you to my parents first and foremost for instilling such a beautiful faith and love of sports in me, and for encouraging me to run after my dreams. To my FIERCE Athlete Team and Board Members for supporting me. To Angelina, for inspiring me to write this so many years ago. To all those that read, endorsed, and helped edit, especially Kate. Finally, thank you to all the female athletes out there who inspire me daily to do what I do! God Bless you all.

Cover Photo: A good friend of mine, Tracy Guerrette, after winning the Maine Marathon and qualifying for the Olympic Trials, kneeling in prayer at the finish line, praising and thanking God and offering Him her race and success. A true depiction of what it means to Be FIERCE.

FOREWORD

In this book are the questions I wrestle with daily. Sam gives simple yet powerful exercises to step into the person who God created you to be. Show up, stay present, and apply these tools to your life and I believe you will see a shift in your heart, your mind, your soul, and your body.

I felt like Sam somehow got into my mind and was speaking into my life; the things I question and the situations I'm in. Sam then walks you through a simple yet dynamic way of attacking the struggles in life. She is so relatable and speaks from her own experiences, and gives you simple action steps and things to ponder. She challenges you to go inside and get real with who you are in Christ.

I encourage you to really sit with the topics and questions that she stirs up in your heart. Take the time to really sit with these and reflect over them throughout the day/week/month/year. Take this book to church, take it to the mountains to reflect, take it on a road trip, and reflect on these questions over and over until you realize who God created you to be.

This is not a book to rush through, but rather work through the practice items and keep pulling these practical tools out. It's not a one and done; it's a tool to help you as you continue to walk and grow. Be disciplined and keep showing up. This is a guide I will pull out time and time again to remind me when I forget, to guide me in my thoughts, and to call me higher to be the best version of myself.

- *Brittany Bock, 2x Soccer All-American, 1st Round Draft Pick, 7 year Pro & National Team Member*

INTRODUCTION

"Athletic activity, in fact, highlights not only man's valuable physical activities, but also his intellectual and spiritual capacities. It's not just physical strength and muscular efficiency, but it also has a soul and must show its complete face." -Pope St. John Paul II

If you are an athlete, I can imagine you want to be the best you can be. You want to run the fastest time, swim the fastest split, have the highest batting average, or be the top goal scorer. Whatever your goal may be, as athletes we have this drive in us to perform, to compete, to win. So, what do we do in order to become the best? We practice and we train. We put in hours and hours of practice in order to get faster, stronger, and more skilled. And yet, for many of us, even though we are so familiar with training ourselves physically in our sport, we don't fully understand the depth to which our bodies have meaning. Furthermore, we watch hours of game film, practice visualization, even have mental toughness techniques, and yet we don't understand the depth of the mind and its power and effect on the rest of the body. Many of us don't even think to train our souls. We may go to Church on Sunday, or spend some time in prayer, but do we realize the complexity of the spiritual life, and how that can actually affect our athletic performance?

Here's the reality. You are a human being. And the definition of a human being is that you are a union of body and soul. At the moment of your conception, you were given an eternal soul, and your cells began to grow into the body you have today. The complexity of the human person, with our ability to reason and our free will, reveals how we are made in the image of God. We are a higher being than other creatures. We can think, move, choose, love, laugh, cry, pray, and yes, play sports. What's amazing about the human person is that our body, mind, soul connections actually affect one another. We are a united being, not divided. What this means is what you do to your body affects your soul and vice-versa: what you do to your soul affects your body.

Therefore, if you want to be the best athlete you can be, if you want the X factor that will elevate your performance, then you must start thinking about how you can train all parts of you: your body, your mind, and your soul. The good news is that you already know how to train for a greater good, to push yourself through discomfort to attain a goal or a victory. Now, let's train to become a complete athlete.

This book will contain facts, stories, and also practicals. We're athletes. We like things to do and to practice in order to get better. Take the time to do the practice items, and revisit and do them again because we know that practice leads to growth, and ultimately to victory.

1. WHO WE THINK WE ARE

Before we can talk about becoming something, we first and foremost have to know who we are. I don't know if this ever happens to you, but sometimes I have trouble sleeping. I toss and turn and can't sleep because I feel like I can't shut off my mind. I become stressed out about life and start thinking about those deeper life questions. Why do they always hit us when we are trying to fall asleep? It's because everything finally is silent. I am no longer distracted by the tasks of the day, the latest text conversation, social media, advertisements, Netflix, other people, music, etc. It's just me, the dark, and my thoughts. That is when those deep questions begin to pervade my mind. Questions like, who am I? What the heck am I doing with my life? What am I supposed to be doing with my life? What does it mean to be a woman? What does it mean to be a man? Am I doing a good job? Am I a good person? What about that thing I did? *Is there more to life than my sport? Who am I without my sport?*

When those questions come to us late at night, what do we usually do though? Do we think about them? No. We roll over in bed, mistakenly thinking that a new position, or a fresh side of the pillow will somehow make those thoughts poof out of existence. When that doesn't work, we pull out our phone, begin scrolling, seeking distraction in some form of entertainment. The truth is these are the questions that make us uncomfortable. They put a knot in our stomachs or seem beyond reach. So, we ignore them, or at least attempt to. But here is the interesting thing. These questions are the most important things we should be contemplating. They are the most fundamental to what it means to be a human person. And yet, we don't think about them, nor do we talk about them. So, guess what? That's exactly where I want to start. I want to start off by discussing who we are. Because before we can grow into the best athlete possible, we have to start off by knowing who it is that is doing the growing, and why.

Where Does My Identity Come From?

So, who are you? You, reader, athlete, who are you? And how is it that you came to define yourself in that way?

Where do you get your identity from? What are some of the things that you look to, in order to decide what it is to be human, to be a woman, to be an athlete?

Your Parents

Our parents, or those that raised us, are really the foundation of our human identity formation, and our self-image. They are the ones to literally name us, and to begin to raise us and form us. Our self-concept, our self-image, even the sport we play, emerged from our family of origin. My dad played college soccer, and my mom was a tri-varsity athlete in high school. I grew up in an athletic family, and my athleticism was ingrained in me, and also modeled for me in my upbringing. Furthermore, the love of our parents is what shows us the worth that we have. Now for some of us, we have a great relationship with our parents. They are the reason we are so confident, successful, supported. But we also know that no parent is perfect. Maybe you grew up in a single parent home. Maybe your parents got divorced. Maybe you felt you had to earn the love of your parents, or they only accepted you if you played well in your game or got straight A's. All these things can have negative effects on our self-image. How did your parents, or guardians, shape you and your beliefs about who you are?

Your Siblings

From a young age, our siblings help teach us who we are. If you had an older sibling you looked up to, a lot of what you did was what they did; I was out playing sports in the neighborhood with my older brother. Maybe they were your biggest fans and support. My sister Jill and I overlapped and played varsity soccer together for three years. She was the goalie, and I was her center defender. I fought to defend the goal, but more so to defend and fight for her. We pushed each other toward our Division 1 soccer dreams. Perhaps, it was your siblings who labeled you in certain ways though, made fun of you, made you question your own worth. Maybe you felt like you always had to compete with your siblings for attention, accolades, or accomplishments. Maybe you felt like you didn't measure up to them and got less attention from them or your parents because of it. No sibling is perfect, and like our parents or other members of our family, they did help shape us and our self-image in both positive and negative ways.

Your Friends and Teammates

They say you can tell a lot about a person from the five people they hang out with most. Our peers, whether from our teams, jobs, or school, heavily influence our sense of self. Some of us look around and we see people that push us to be better. We see people that accept us just for who we are. We seem to be cut from the same cloth. It's taken a long time, but these are the people I strive to be around most. But all of us have had some tough friendships. I think friendship wounds are one of the hardest things to deal with as a young person. We so badly want to fit in, be accepted, be cool, that oftentimes we find ourselves conforming to other people and what they want to do rather than sticking to what we want or know to be the right thing. I get it, I've been there. Peer pressure is real. So sometimes our friends can lead us to become better versions of ourselves, and sometimes we conform and seemingly lose ourselves.

Other Leaders

There are so many others that lead us, and therefore affect us and our identity. Our coaches, teachers, and bosses are among this group. As athletes especially, our coaches can be some of the most influential people in our lives. Their philosophies on sport and coaching can teach us a lot. Also, how they treat us and view us has deep effects. Are we valuable to them beyond our PR (personal record)? My best coaches, I think, found that balance between pushing me and challenging me on the field, ice, or track, but at the same time cared about how I was doing personally. They got to know me. They knew how to push me the way I needed to be pushed and loved in the ways I needed to be loved and reassured. I have also had coaches that I know at times saw me as a commodity. They liked me, paid attention to me if I did well, and if I didn't, I felt hidden and like a let-down. The same has been true in my life with teachers, professors, and bosses. They have both positively and negatively affected my life and how I see myself. We find that these individuals we looked to for guidance can make comments that can really help us believe in ourselves or, on the contrary, really cut painfully deep and hurt our confidence.

Famous Athletes

Most of us have grown up with athletes that we look up to. I loved watching all sports growing up and was so inspired by them. I watched how they played and how they competed, how they handled winning and losing. I paid attention to their statistics and training methods and sought to emulate them. We need this and we can learn so much from watching others who are at the top level of athletics. But we also learn a lot from these athletes' conduct and personal lives. Some athletes are great role models: humble, hardworking, and grateful. Others are prideful, self-indulgent, and headlining for doing illegal or bad things. Their witness can affect how we think we should conduct ourselves on and off the field.

Social Media

Who do you follow on social media? What videos do you find yourself watching? We have to be careful. In today's world, people are putting their "best self" on display for the world to see, whether it be perfect lighting, caption, pose, smile, or "good time". Meanwhile, we find ourselves comparing our lives, our interior, to their seemingly perfect exterior. The result can be comparison, judgment, and jealousy. What we view, and who we follow may help us determine what it is to be "cool", but is that a good thing? Or is it leading you to conform? Or to hate who you are or what you don't have? I recently limited myself to five minutes a day on social media because I realized I was addicted to it. It's where I went when I had a few minutes of idle time, and I was comparing myself to others. My social media now is mostly filled with golden retriever puppy videos and close friends who uplift me and I want to keep in touch with, rather than people I felt I had to compete against or compared myself to.

I also had to check my reason for posting. What a gut check that was. I was posting things because I wanted others to look at my life and think, "Wow, she's cool. She surfs, has a cool Jeep, and just worked out hard." I was looking for the affection of others there. Now if I post, it's mostly of my dog, because others have said it brings them joy. I want to bring others joy and uplift others rather than one-up them.

Media

You may not realize it but what you listen to, and what you watch affect you. How many times have I heard someone listening to hard rap say, "I just like the beat, I'm not listening to the lyrics"? Or "It's just a TV show, I know it's fake, and I won't act like that"? I get it, and I'm not hating-on hard rap or certain tv series. But if you stop to listen to the lyrics, what are they saying? Are they degrading women? Are they cursing? Are the shows we watch over-sexual, bordering on pornographic? Are they extremely violent? These things affect us on a subconscious level even if we don't want to admit it. The subconscious mind makes up 85% of our brains and affects our conscious minds and decisions. And they also affect us on a spiritual level.

Practice Item

Take a moment here to pause and write. Take a self-inventory. Who has helped influence who you think you are and how?

Our Three Origins of Identity

While there are many other things that affect us, I would argue that we can actually categorize the ways we let these influences define us. I think we come to define ourselves in three ways, and each of the ways actually sets us up for failure. The three ways are:

1. What we do
2. What we look like
3. Others' opinions of us

What we do

Let's start with what we do. Does what you do matter? Yes. It's awesome that you're on the women's hockey team or an All-American discus thrower. That's amazing! But, if you base your identity just off the fact that you're a starter on your college basketball team, what happens if you get hurt? What happens if you don't start? What happens if you don't have a good game? Then you might start to believe the lie: "If I don't do _____ (fill in the blank), I won't be liked", or "I'm not worthy of love", or "I'm not worth it".

"If I don't get an A on my test, then I'm worthless. If I don't make varsity, then I am a loser." We all have a script, or more likely multiple scripts, in our head. If we don't do something, we feel like we're worthless. The reality is we are not perfect, and we do not reach our goals due to a whole range of circumstances. As a result, we end up setting ourselves up for failure. And the result is we degrade our own efforts, pursuits, and our very selves.

What we look like

The next is what we look like. I know this is especially particular to us women (though men are not exempt from this by any means). From a woman's perspective though, I think all of us have this ideal in our mind of what beauty is. For me it was always tall, blond, and skinny. I've got the height, as I'm 6 feet tall, but I've got these massive soccer thighs. I'm not skinny. And I'm not blond. I guess I could dye my hair. But the point is, we create these statements in our minds, "Well if only I was skinny, if only I lost 10 pounds, if only _____ (fill in the blank), then I would be beautiful, or I would be lovable, or I would get attention from that guy." Do you see how these things, again, set us up for failure?

I recently came upon the social media profile of one of the best college female soccer players in the country. I would have thought her photos would have been of her playing soccer, but instead they were mostly of her posing in a bikini. Now is she beautiful? Yes, absolutely (we all are), but why did she feel like she had to pose that way in front of her tens of thousands of followers?

Does what she and you look like matter? Yeah. We're going to talk about that, but if we base our sole identity just on what we look like, then it ends up really confusing our sense of self and oftentimes leads us to compensate, flaunt, or even hate our bodies.

Others' opinions of us

The last thing that we base our identity on is others' opinions of us; coaches, parents, friends, even people we don't know on social media or in the stands, etc. We discussed this earlier. Do their opinions matter? Yes and no. We need to listen to our coaches and teammates and follow what they say. But for me, a lot of times when I was playing college soccer, if I played well in practice, and my coach praised me, it was a great day. If I got critiqued by him, or my teammates didn't want to hang out, or I heard some backhand comment from one of them, how did I feel? Like I didn't matter. The statement becomes "If I do _____, then my teammates will like me", or "If my coach _____, then I know I have worth on this team." Again, those people's opinions of us can matter, but if we base our identity on what they think or what they say, then we set ourselves up for failure.

Additionally, we end up giving in and doing something that we are not comfortable with in order to fit in. In the moment this may make us feel like we have worth, but in the end, we lose sight of ourselves and end up lost or miserable. I can't tell you how many times this happened to me, especially in college. "Well, I am the only person on my team who doesn't drink, so I guess I'll try it in order to fit in." In the end, every time I would feel miserable and less like myself.

Practice Item

Make a list. Where do I put my identity and how have I seen that hurt me or set me up for failure? What are the "If only I _____, then _____" statements that I have formed?

2. WHO WE ACTUALLY ARE

When we think about identity, we think it's what makes us different and unique from everyone else, but interestingly the root of the word identity is actually the Latin word *idem* which means "the same". What then, is "the same" about all of us? The answer can actually be found in scripture. I love scripture. I see the Bible like God's playbook. He lays out clearly how to execute the game of life. It's all right there! In regards to our identity, scripture says two things about our "sameness". The first can be found in Genesis 1:27. It states, "So God created man in his own image, in the image of God he created him; male and female he created them" (NRSV). We are all made in God's image and likeness. That's what distinguishes us as human beings from animals. Secondly, in 2 Corinthians 6:18, it states "'and I will be a father to you, and you shall be my sons and daughters, says the Lord Almighty'" (NRSV). We are God's adopted sons and daughters. That is your core identity. That YOU ARE A DAUGHTER OF GOD. You've probably heard that before. "Yeah, I know, I'm a daughter of God". But have you ever really internalized it? As athletes, we're doers. I don't know about you, but I was always going a million miles an hour. I still am, but here is the reality, (in fact, perhaps the most real thing you can take from this whole book); If you sat in the chair you're currently sitting in while you read this book for the rest of your life and did nothing, just sat there, God would love you the same as if you went on to make the Olympic team, win a gold medal, or win the Nobel Peace Prize. No matter what you do or don't do, God still loves you the exact same.

If you sat in a chair for the rest of your life and did nothing, God would love you just the same.

That is where your true identity lies. You are loved just as you are. It is not conditional. It is not contingent on your performance, or what you do, or don't do. You are loved unconditionally as God's Daughter. The God who created the universe, the earth, everything around you, loves you for you, as you are. When I came to realize that truth in my own life...everything changed.

My Story

If you had asked me in high school who I was, I would have responded quickly and proudly, "an athlete". I was a nine-time state champion in high school. I won an ice hockey state championship, seven track state championships, including individually in the hurdles and 3x in the triple jump, and won a soccer state championship. Even though I was more highly recruited for track in college, it was always my dream to play Division 1 soccer, and I jumped at the opportunity to go to the University of Connecticut (UConn). I was from Connecticut, so being recruited as a hometown kid was a big deal, and UConn was a top-25 program. So here I am, so ready to go, and what do I do? Tear my ACL, my LCL, and my meniscus in a soccer game my senior year of high school. They actually told me I'd never play again, but I am pretty stubborn and resilient. It was three surgeries and 13 months before I set foot on a soccer field, and about three years to actually come back and play at a competitive D1 level again.

So here I am. I show up to UConn as a freshman, and I'm not playing but sitting on the bench. Everything was different. School was different, my friends and family were gone, and I couldn't play my sport. Suddenly the girl who considered herself "an athlete" first and foremost didn't know who she was. So, I began to try and discover my identity. Where did I turn? I turned to what my teammates thought of me. I started partying with them. I turned to what my coach thought of me. I started to change who I was because I was just trying to figure it out. And was I successful? No, I was miserable. But like most of us athletes, we know how to put up a tough front. We know how to perform and smile, and we know how to maintain a 3.9 GPA in the honors program and double major while doing so. Nobody knew from the outside. But interiorly, I was growing more and more depressed, hopeless, and lost.

Fast forward to my junior year. I was at UConn in early August for pre-season and my team and I are some of the only people on campus. It's 95 degrees out with two-a-day practices plus conditioning, film, and daily meetings. It's a lot. During the middle of pre-season, a Sunday came around, and I just wanted a little break. We'd been there for over a week, and I was like, "I need to get away from my team, what can I do?" I was like, "I'll go to Mass. I'm Catholic and kind of into Mass. I'll go to Mass. My coach will let me do that." Long story short, I ended up going to Mass to escape pre-season. And I made sure to bring my "athlete water bottle" with me (if you are a college athlete, you know this is the sure sign on campus you're an athlete), so that everyone at Mass would know why I showed up in sweats, just happy to sit and be alone in air conditioning for an hour.

I had grown up Catholic. My mom was very faithful, and we would go to Mass as a family on the weekends, even sometimes daily during Lent, and would pray an occasional family rosary. But as I got to college, I'd only go to Mass when it was convenient, or I wasn't traveling or busy with soccer. But that hot August day, God used an excuse to begin to change my life. There was this girl at Mass, one of the only other young people there. Because it was before the school year had started, I was the only student there amidst an older local population. Anyway, this girl gets up to do the readings at Mass, and I remember thinking to myself, "Who the heck does this girl think she is?" Yeah, I was a punk. But what I couldn't name then, was that this girl so apparently had the joy I was so desperately seeking. It radiated from her. In how she spoke, in her smile, in how she bounced when she walked. That same girl came up to me after Mass, seeing the "labeling" athlete water bottle and asked if I was an athlete and then proceeded to ask me about myself. I went back to Mass the next week just to see that girl. And there she was and again she talked to me, remembering my name. Her name was Angel. Go figure. I came to find out she was a missionary and she asked me to join her bible study that fall. I agreed.

At this point, I was willing to try anything. So, that entire fall I sat quietly and quite intimidated in a bible study with a group of women who seemed to have it all together. Meanwhile, I was still spiraling.

Later that winter, Angel literally punked me into going to a conference in Florida. I had told her "No" four times, but on the fifth ask, she revealed she had saved money for me to go since the day she met me. It was a total guilt trip. I actually began to cry, and I, the "tough athlete" didn't cry. Angel's response, "Aren't those tears probably a sign you should go?" She knew I couldn't back down from a challenge.

Well, it worked, and it was perhaps one of the most important "yesses" I've ever given. I showed up at this conference and there were thousands of other college students alive in their faith. They were joyful and excited to be there. So, after the opening mass (realizing I wasn't so excited but wanted to be) I surrendered and said to God, "Ok God, I am here for four days, do with me what you want." It was a prayer far bolder and inviting than I realized. I had opened myself to God, just a crack, and He used that crack to enter into my life. A few days later I felt called to go to Confession for the first time in a long time. And finally, I felt like I was actually honest and raw with both the priest and myself about the ways I had turned away from

God. The priest's and ultimately Christ's forgiveness was so gentle and so tangible, it left me feeling new and fresh. That night we had something called Adoration. I don't know if you've ever been to Adoration, but in the Catholic faith, it is when we take the Body of Christ in the host and put him on display in something called a monstrance, to pray before. Angel had brought me to adoration the night before and I just sat there unphased. But that night, as a procession entered the room, with a priest holding the monstrance, I got the chills. As the priest drew closer, my whole body began to shake. Then when the priest was right behind me, I looked up into the monstrance, and I saw Jesus. I saw who and what I had been longing for, for so long. With every fiber of my being, I knew that that was Christ, and I was overcome with inexplicable joy and for the first time in my life I began to weep out of joy. Every doubt, question, and depressed feeling I'd bottled over the last three years was gone.

For years, I had believed that my identity lay in what I did or didn't do. I viewed myself as a failure, and suddenly when I encountered the Lord, I knew that I wasn't loved because I was some stud soccer player or a 3.9 student or whatever. I was loved just for who I was. That changed everything, because then it gave me the freedom to accept the gifts that God had given me, and who He had created me to be. I had found truth and meaning, and my response as an athlete had to be, "I am all in". Everything had to, and did, change in my life for the better.

Practice Item

Reflect on my story, and then your own. Have you had a similar encounter with God? What is the story of your journey of faith? Do you know God personally? If you haven't encountered Him, ask Him to reveal Himself in your life.

Our Gifts

Identity is a paradox. Our faith is full of seeming paradoxes. Identity is what unites us all, but it's also what makes us unique. It's where our God-given gifts lay. Think about this for a second, how many people are in the world right now? There's around 7.8 billion people on the earth right now, and there have been billions of people that have existed before, right? We don't know when the Lord's going to come again and the world is going to end, but potentially there will be billions and billions of more people, and in all those billions of people before, now, and to come, there has never been nor will ever be somebody else who looks exactly like you do...unless you're an identical twin (haha.). But follow me further. There is no other person that has existed, exists, or will exist that looks like you do, has your gifts, your talents, your dreams, your desires, your little quirks. You are completely and utterly unique. What's more, remember how I said earlier that what distinguishes us is that we're made in God's image and likeness? Well, if we're made in God's image and likeness, and we are completely unique, then that means that you reveal something unique about God that nobody else does.

> You reveal something unique about God that nobody else does.

You reveal something about God both in how you look, and in who you are. A really funny person points to God's humor. A really compassionate person points to His compassionate heart. An artistic person points to God's creative action and love. The artist's heart is revealed in his artwork. It says something about him or her. Well, you are God's masterpiece! The height of His creation. A specific artistic rendering of a piece of Him. That means that when someone looks at you, they see a piece of God. When you look at someone else, you encounter and learn something new about God. This is one of the reasons sports are so amazing. When you compete against other people, when you look at them, play against them, witness them doing something remarkably athletic with their bodies, you are seeing God's handiwork. In sport, the body is the artform.

But do we view ourselves like that? Do we view others like that? Do we view our gifts and talents like that? Specifically, since I'm talking about athletics, do you view your athletic talent as a gift? As something you've been given as a gift to reveal God?

We know that our identity is in that we are sons and daughters of God. The way that we live that out is through the gifts and talents that we've been given. Again, does God love you because you play a sport? He doesn't love you because of that, but he loves that about you. He made you with those athletic gifts. I liken it to a story in my college career. We were in the Big East Conference at the time, so we were traveling all over the country. My parents would tag team games because my sister was playing D1 soccer as well, but my dad only missed four away games in my college career. That includes the three and a half years that I sat on the bench. I played for five years, and I got to eventually be captain and start and play. But even when I wasn't playing, he would come watch me warm up. Why? He just delighted in me and what I was a part of. Now, when I became captain and was starting, did my dad delight in the fact that I was playing? Yes, but did he love me more because of it? No. That is Our Father's love. His love for you doesn't change whether you play or not; he doesn't love you for what you study, or for all the incredible things you do, but He does delight in them. Your gifts, the talents, desires, and dreams that you have, God gave those to you. And using your gifts well is a way that only you can honor and thank him.

When we receive a present, what do we want to do with it? Open it and use it. Use it to its full potential. That is what God desires for us and our athletic talent.

Practice Item:

Reflect on your uniqueness and your unique gifts. What are your gifts? What are your gifts outside your athletic talent? (Yes there is more to you than that!) What do you, and your gifts reveal about God? How are you being called to honor God with your gifts?

Who is God?

But if we are made in God's image and likeness, and He gave us all these gifts, like our athleticism, and we reflect Him...well, who is God? Growing up I saw God as this authoritarian figure, sitting up in the clouds, pointing out all the things I had done wrong. Cue lightning bolt! But the reality is that God is a loving Father. For some of us, that can be hard to imagine, because perhaps our own fathers weren't loving, and we can project that onto God. But His love and who He is, is far beyond what we can comprehend.

I want to tell you a story. It's a love story actually, and one that I think reveals why God is a loving Father. It's a story you have heard before, but I hope as you read you will listen as if for the first time. The story starts with a young woman around 14-16 years old. An angel appears to this woman and asks her if she is willing to have the Son of God. Not by an earthly husband, but by God Himself in the Holy Spirit. So, the God who created this woman, then asks her permission to have His Son be conceived in her womb. She says yes, and so the God who created the universe, chooses to become one of His creatures: a baby. A baby that needs to grow, be birthed, be fed, and have His diaper changed. The gravity of that is like you or I choosing to become a little ant, but times infinity. So, this baby, the God of the universe, is born into utter poverty, in a dirty smelly stable. He then has to flee with His parents because there is a hit out on His life. He returns from Egypt years later, and the only time we really catch a glimpse of Him, is when He's twelve and is one-upping some scholars in the temple after His parents "lose" him. Other than that, this Son of God, grows up silently, learning scripture, helping around the house, and working in His father's trade as a carpenter.

Thirty years later, He emerges onto the scene after turning water into wine at a wedding per his mother's request. He then gathers twelve friends and goes camping with them for three years, teaching, leading, guiding, and forming them. He begins to work miracles for the people: curing disease, making the blind see, casting out demons, and even raising people from the dead. And as His followers grow, so does His opposition. And one day, he hosts a last dinner, in which He gives His friends His very self in the bread and wine as His Body and Blood, and commands they carry that on. After, He is arrested. He is betrayed and sold out by one of His apostles, one of His closest friends. They come and find Him in a garden where He is arrested while praying. While praying for you, and for me, while seeing our sin, and what is about to happen to Him. He is sweating blood because of the depth of distress. He is seized, shackled, imprisoned, dragged to court, flogged gruesomely to the point where His skin hangs in flaps from His body. Any normal person would have died then, but this Man was choosing His moment. He was then crowned with thorns, which consisted of two-inch thorns that were stabbed into

His scalp. He was mocked and spat at. Then He was made to march uphill 800m (if you are a track athlete, you know that may be the most grueling race), with a heavy 75lb-125lb cross on his back. He is thirsty, bloody, tired, cramping, and having trouble breathing. He falls, not once, not twice, but three times. And each time He gets back up because He is determined to finish what He started and achieve what He set out for.

When He reaches the top of the hill, He is then stripped completely naked. His arms and legs are outstretched, which requires multiple men to pull on because they are so cramped up, and His hands and feet are nailed to the cross. Then He is lifted up, for all to see, as a mockery. The position of His body on the cross, arms extended makes breathing become increasingly difficult. In fact, to breathe you have to lift yourself up, on your nailed hands and feet. So, to breathe is excruciating; to speak is beyond comprehension. And yet this man, Jesus, chooses to say a few things while hanging on that cross. One of them is "'Woman, behold, your son!' Then he said to the disciple, 'Behold your mother!'" (John 19:26b-27a NRSV). God again asks the woman to become a mother. In the height of her suffering, watching the One she loves most be tortured and die, He asks her to mother the very people killing Him: us. God gives us a gift, a mother, a woman, Mary, who we will discuss later in this book. She is our perfect model. Additionally, He says, "Father, forgive them for they know not what they do." This is the clincher, the giveaway. You see, when Adam and Eve disobeyed God, a rupture was created because of our sin. We could no longer be in perfect relationship with God. The wage of that sin was death (Romans 6:23). And God, who is a loving Father, and who couldn't stand not being in a relationship with us, sent his Son, to take on our sin, and die for us, even though He was innocent and never sinned. Jesus, on the cross proclaims, "It is finished" (John 19:30) and He dies.

But that's not the end of the story. He descends into hell, beats Satan, and then RISES FROM THE DEAD. He conquers death. He endures the most brutal death, abandonment, betrayal, and rejection that ever existed, because He wanted to be back in relationship with you. And there is the reality. If you were the only person that existed God would

> If you were the only person that existed, God would have done the same thing.

have done the same thing. He did it with you in mind- you with your smile, your soccer thighs, the scar on your knee, your quirks, even your sins. He did that because He loved you. He loves you. He forgives you. That is who God is. That is who you reflect. That is the depth of your worth.

Now the decision is yours. Are you willing to open your heart to the God who went to His death so he could know you, talk with you, be a part of your life?

Practice Item

Reflect on the story you just heard. How did it strike your heart? Do you believe God did this for you? Pray a simple prayer such as *"Jesus thank you for dying for me, I accept you as my Savior. I open my life to you. Please come into my heart, my athletic career, my family, relationships, dreams, and life. Bless me and help me reflect you."*

So now that we know WHO we are, we want to talk about how to live that out. How to be the best human we can be, and how to be the best athlete we can be. Let's together jump into how to live out our life as a human person, as an athletic human person from a physical perspective looking at our bodies, from a mental perspective tying in psychology, and then from a spiritual perspective looking at how our interior life drives us.

3. PHYSICALLY

Our view v. God's view

As human beings we are a union of body and soul. What we do to our souls affects our bodies and what we do to our bodies affects our souls. So, when addressing how to grow as a whole human person, to be a complete athlete, it's important to consider and address the physical, the body. God designed your body. He cares about it.

What is the one thing that every athlete uses, no matter the sport, equipment needs, environment, etc., when they play or compete in their sport? The body. And what do we think of our bodies? What is our particular view of our bodies as athletes? Well depending on the person, education, sport, and external factors, I think we have a lot of different views. For some of us, we view the body as a kind of tool to be used. There's this NFL player that was quoted saying how his body was a well-oiled machine. He knew that if he did squats and lifted and ran extra sprints, his body was going to get stronger and faster. He said it was such a well-oiled machine that he almost felt disassociated from it. This is because it became just something that he used and that he manipulated in order to perform better on the field. As a result, he didn't view it as united to his soul, as an intimate part of his being. This is a common temptation to fall into. It is remarkable how our bodies respond to different forms of training, and we do need to work hard to improve our speed, vertical jump, performance, and skills. However, it must always be done in a way that reverences and does not separate us from our bodies, but more deeply unites us with them.

Another view is that some of us might look at our athletic bodies, and we might have a lot of pride in them. Maybe we idolize our bodies. We flaunt them. We know that we're fit, and we look good, and we use them for attention. Now, we will get into the fact that the body is good, but if we're using it to get the attention of others it's a slightly twisted way of looking at the body. This does relate to how we dress. It's ok to wear clothes that aid your performance and help you function better when competing. However, off the court or outside the pool, we should dress in a way that doesn't flaunt our bodies in order to draw attention to them. Rather, we are called to accent the beauty that we already possess as athletic women.

Still another view is one I personally fell into. I'm six feet tall, pretty muscular, and I always thought that I was unfeminine because I looked a certain way. I thought I looked, or was too, masculine. It led to body hate and body shame. And whether it's because we view our bodies as too masculine, or not attractive, or not like others by comparison, body shame and body hate is a deep and very common wound for women. We're constantly critiquing how we look. What was the last thing you said to yourself when you looked in the mirror? If you're like me, it was probably some self-critique or negative remark.

Practice Item

What is your view of your athletic body? Can you relate to the views above?

The Goodness of Our Bodies

This isn't God's intention for the view of our bodies, especially because as athletes we're so, so familiar with them. It's crazy how in tune we have become with our bodies and how they are feeling. We know when we have tweaked a muscle or when we are just sore. We know when we can push through pain and when we need to stop. We know when a cold is coming, or we feel off. It's beautiful. And yes, we know when we need surgery. Case in point – and this is actually kind of funny – but I was recently playing pickleball with my parents, who I refer to as Mr. and Mrs. Pickleball of America. There is no question where I get my athletic talent from. They seriously kick my butt when we play. They go to pickleball camps, train daily, and enter tournaments. It's a whole thing. Anyway, I love playing with them and one day I take this overhead swing for a ball, and I pop my shoulder. Immediately I knew I had torn my labrum. I just knew. Seventh surgery here we come. We know our bodies.

We
know
our
bodies.

We know our bodies so well. We know when they're good and rested and healthy, and we know when they're hurt, but I think we fail to see the true goodness of them and the true purpose of them. I want you all to just look down at your body for a second. *Behold it is very good.* You may smile, chuckle, or feel really uncomfortable at that. Even shrug it off with "well not my body", or "if only" statements we talked about earlier. But here is the reality: our bodies are not just good; *they are very good.* Let's look at the creation of not just them, but of the whole world. In the book of Genesis, the first book of the Bible, lies the story of creation. It says, God took seven days to create the world (well, six and on the seventh He rested). Over the first six days God creates light and dark, the sun, moon and stars, the ocean, all creatures, sunsets, beautiful mountains, flowers - everything you see. And after He creates all those things, what does he say? "Behold, it is good." Then God creates the human person, the human body, man and woman. He looks at all He created and what does he say? "Behold, it is *very* good." Do you see the small difference? Good v. very good? Have you ever thought about the significance of that? It's a small difference but it has a vast effect. That means that your body and my body are

Your body and my body are more sacred, beautiful, good, and holy than the rest of creation.

37

more sacred, beautiful, good, and holy than the rest of creation- better than the Northern lights, Mount Everest, Fiji, a sunset on the beach, the most beautiful flower you've ever seen, Golden Retriever puppies or whatever your image is of beauty. It's incredible! We are the crown of His creation. Do we view our bodies like that? Do we view others' bodies like that?

If we're honest, not usually, no. We're riddled with critique and self-hate. A friend has a little six-year-old girl who's in ballet class. One class, the instructor had all the little five and six-year-olds, in their little tutus, walk up to the mirror and say one thing that they liked about themselves. I love this. What an amazing teacher. But this one little girl walks up to the mirror, and she stands there, and then after some time she just begins to cry. At six years old she could not think of one thing that she liked about herself. What did this girl hear at home? Who made her think at six years old that she was not good and beautiful? And how much older are you? How many more years of comments by people and comparisons to other women, and being ignored by men have you had to destroy your self-image?

And you're not alone. Dove soap did a study a number of years ago, and they found that 96% of women do not think that they are beautiful.[1] 96%. That is shocking

38

in some ways, but I know it to be true. It's an epidemic. As women we are particularly attacked in this area, in how we view ourselves. But in order to be the best we can be as athletes, and more so beyond that, as women, we need to realize our true worth. I heard a coach say men need to win in order to feel good, and women need to feel good in order to win. I want to help you realize that you are the crown of creation.

Practice Item

Part 1. The body scan. What I want you to do is to sit somewhere quietly, and I want you to start at the top of your head and go body part by body part down your whole body to your toes, and I want you to ask yourself, "Do I like this part of my body?" (Do I like my hair? Do I like my forehead? My eyebrows? My eyes? etc.) *Do this now. Seriously. Put the book down and go for it!*

How was it? It's pretty brutal. The first time I did it, I probably critiqued about 80% of my body. Eighty percent. Whether it be my frizzy hair, former unibrow, pig nose, stomach. I critiqued it. I will say I do like my legs though. Ladies, I've done a lot of squats for those legs! There is some healthy pride in how hard I've trained. But overall, we all have a sense of body shame. However, I don't want you to stop there.

Part 2. Now I want you to either go to the chapel or just close your eyes and picture God. Picture Him however you want, whether it be God the Father, or Jesus as an infant or on the Cross or Resurrected. Put yourself in His presence and see Him look at you, and then I want you to do the body scan from the top of your head to the bottom of your toes again, and this time with every body part I want you to ask the Lord, ask Jesus, "Lord, do you love this part of my body?" Hint: His answer is always, "Yes." Do this now. *Trust me, we all need to hear what He has to say to start healing our self-image.*

"Yes, Samantha, I love your little pig nose that you used to get made fun of for. I love the fact that you're six feet tall. I love your soccer thighs and rowing shoulders." Whatever it is, let Him show you how He sees you, how He created you, how He loves you. This is practically how we can come to love our bodies, come to see ourselves the way that our Creator sees us. He wants to heal your physical self-image. Now, I'll do this body scan and I only critique about 20% of my body. It's a journey, but by doing this exercise regularly I have come a long way since 80% and you can too.

Someone to Honor

But God so loves our bodies, that He decides to take his love for us one giant step further. He dwells in us. In 1 Corinthians 6:19-20 it says, "Or do you not know that your body is a temple of the Holy Spirit within you, which you have from God, and that you are not your own? For you were bought with a price; therefore, glorify God in your body." (NRSV) What do you think of when you think of a temple? Or a church? How would you describe a church or a temple?

Is it dirty? No. It's nice and clean. It's pure. Is it ugly? No, it's beautiful, magnificent, and draws the heart toward heaven. Is it profane? No, it's sacred, and holy. When we are baptized, the Trinity comes to dwell in us, in the depths of our hearts and our souls. Our bodies become living temples. Do we treat our bodies like that? As pure, beautiful, and sacred? As athletes we know that how we treat our bodies matters for our overall performance. First and foremost, how much you sleep matters. Sleep is the number one reducer of cortisol, the stress hormone. Sleep and periods of rest and recovery from intense training are very important for our overall bodily and spiritual health. Above all else, sleep needs to be prioritized, and as athletes you should be getting 8-10 hours a night!

Secondly, what you eat matters. Nutrition is our fuel. Every body, depending on its type and type of working out, needs different amounts and types of nutrition. There is no blanket diet. However, pay attention to what you are fueling your temple with. The vast majority of foods are processed, have added sugars, and unnatural ingredients. Just look at the labels. These do not help our bodies function to their full potential.

Thirdly, what you do on the weekend or in your off-time matters. It affects your performance, but more than that it affects your bodies, and it affects your souls. Drinking underage or excessively distorts your reason and has negative effects on your life and is a large factor in falling into impurity. Now if you have been there, the mercy of God is vast, and you should seek forgiveness and the sacrament of Confession. But when we think about how God dwells in us, we realize He is present in all our activities. It is a good rule of thumb when we are choosing what to do in our free time to ask, "Would God want to do this or see this?" Are you honoring and glorifying Him with your choices?

Finally, and as athletes you are already doing this, staying physically active is important. The health benefits are great, and so even after we retire, though it's not necessary or even healthy to maintain our elite working out status, we do need to move regularly and establish a sustainable habit of staying active. Treat your body as if it is a house you are going to live in for the next 70 years. How true that is, and yet it is more than a house, it is God's temple!

I would like to make a note about bodily injuries. Injuries are a part of sport. When we push our bodies to the limits they can break, tear, sprain, get sore etc. Oftentimes no matter how much we have taken care of our bodies and rested, these things can be out of our control. I have had 6, soon to be 7 orthopedic surgeries since my senior year of high school: 4 knees, a hip, and now two shoulders. It's not fun and it is a result of the fall of Adam and Eve and humanity. Our bodies are mortal, and they can get hurt. But just because our bodies are fallen, doesn't make them bad. Again, we want to care for our injuries and strike a balance when competing by not pushing them too hard, but things happen. This is an

> Just because our bodies are fallen, doesn't make them bad.

opportunity to rest and recover, and with hard work come back even stronger. We will discuss later how you can use your injury for good. But for now, make peace with where your body is, and rather than dwell on the injury, look at all of the amazing things it has allowed you to do.

This overall view of our body and how to take care of it should cause a shift. But we need to test our motivation behind taking care of ourselves. I'll use an example: you want to lose 10lbs. First of all, I would ask, "Why?". Is it like we talked about in the beginning of this book, because then you will view yourself as beautiful? I promise that even if you get there, it won't make you feel beautiful. Empty rather. If it is because you want to be healthier or for your performance, then we can do so responsibly. But know this...you are already perfect, sacred, holy, and loved as you are. You do not need to change. Here is your motivation:

YOU ARE NOT SOMETHING TO FIX.
YOU ARE SOMEONE TO HONOR.

You are not something to fix. You are very good as you are. You are not something to fix. You are someone to honor. Do you see the shift there from the negative to the positive? The reason you're taking care of yourself or losing 10lbs (if that is still what you think you need,) isn't because there's something wrong with you. There is nothing wrong with you. You are doing it because you are someone who's been created uniquely and preciously, and your body is good, and so those things matter. And you can judge your motivation by its fruits. If we approach change from the negative – "I'm something to fix" – the fruits of that motivation are fear, anxiety, shame, and fad diets that we give up and quit on. When we approach it from the positive – "I'm someone to honor" – it brings freedom, joy, peace, and results.

Practice Item

"You are not something to fix, you are someone to honor." How does this statement change my motivation for taking care of myself? Where do I need to shift my motivation to a positive honoring of my body? Am I taking care of myself in all the physical spheres talked about?

Our Bodies Reveal Our Souls

The really cool thing about our bodies too is that they don't just exist. They aren't just here, with no deeper meaning. They actually reveal something about us and about

God! Why did God create differences? Why did He create two sexes? What does that reveal about us?

As athletes, you can walk around campus or even in public and you can pretty easily pick out another athlete by how they look. By how they walk, carry themselves, and move. Furthermore, you can often tell what sport somebody plays by how their body looks. I'm an abnormally tall soccer player, so that was a bit of an anomaly. But you know who the basketball and volleyball players are, typically because of their size. You know the swimmers, their bodies reveal a little bit of a T-shape because of their really strong shoulders and arms. Specialists in different strokes and distance swimmers even look different, specific to their event. Distance runners tend to be lean and slight. Your bodies respond to and reveal how you train. Similarly, our bodies reveal our souls and how we're supposed to live. Women, your body actually reveals what the height of your femininity is, and men's bodies reveal the height of their masculinity.

Men's and women's bodies are different, and that difference reveals the difference between masculinity and femininity. Let's start with men and their masculinity. In the sexual act men are external and have the role of the giver. They offer their bodies to the woman. They give themselves. They sacrifice. Because our bodies and souls are connected, this actually reveals that the height of their masculinity is sacrifice. Why do men grow up liking superheroes and movies like Braveheart? Something in them desires to sacrifice for a greater good for another. Who is their ultimate example? Who are they

> The height
> of
> masculinity
> is sacrifice.

called to model their lives after? Who lived out his masculinity perfectly? Jesus on the Cross. Jesus had to be a man because in His masculinity, He offered Himself. He sacrificed himself, body, and soul. Literally every time men play their sport, they have an opportunity to really live out their masculinity, sacrificing themselves for their teammates and sacrificing their bodies. And as we expand beyond sport, that can look all sorts of ways. It can be as a husband sacrificing by going to work every day. It can be as a soldier. It can be as simple as opening a door for a woman. There are so many ways that men can live out that call towards sacrifice. Unfortunately, we more often see men fall short of this call to sacrifice. Instead, we see them live out a spirit of dominance. Whether that be toward other men and their teammates, or even women. There are ways in which we, as women, can call them higher and invite them to live out sacrifice. For example, yes you have arms (and I bet strong ones at that), but if you let a man open a door for you, you are allowing him in a small way to live as he was created to be. We can inspire the men around us to be who they were created to be, in how we carry ourselves as women in the height of our femininity.

For us women, our sexual organs are internal, and we're receptive, we receive the man, and then we have this crazy ability to literally grow life within us and birth and sustain it. The height of our femininity is actually receptivity and then bearing forth and nurturing life. Why did we love princess movies growing up? We wanted to be received and sacrificed for by a prince. But as an adult, I love Wonder Woman. She's a total BA, but there are still parts of her that are still very receptive to others. There is a scene in the movie Wonder Woman, where she encounters suffering for the first time, as she sees the wounded soldiers coming back from the battle front. And in this moment, she doesn't become hysterical, rather her voice drops, she receives the pain of those people, and she utters "It's awful." She is an example of the fierceness and tenderness of a woman. And who is our perfect model of femininity? Who lived out her

> The height of femininity is receptivity and then bearing forth and nurturing life.

femininity perfectly? Mary. Literally, an angel comes to her and says, "Will you have the Son of God?" And what does she do? She's receptive, and she says yes – "fiat" – thus bearing forth life. Taking it deeper, I love how you really see her receptivity lived out perfectly at the foot of the cross. Think about the person that you love most being tortured and killed in front of you. What does she do? She stands there to console Him. She stands and receives her Son with strength and consoles Him. And then Jesus asks something of her again. He asks her to become the mother of the very people killing him, of all of humanity, and in the height of her suffering she's receptive again to God and says "yes." I think women's ability to say yes, to receive others, and to bear forth new life in the midst of suffering is truly remarkable.

Now, I always believed the lie that I wasn't feminine, because I was athletic and I loved sports, but actually the simple fact that I was created a woman makes me feminine. I am going to say that again, because we have to be so important with our language these days. I was not unfeminine- the fact that I was created biologically as a woman

The fact that I was created biologically as a woman, makes me feminine.

makes me feminine. I am feminine in my whole being, body and soul. You cannot separate the body and soul. I know our culture says you can, and can choose whatever body or soul you want, but you literally cannot separate them. That's how you've been created. God did not make a mistake. You can reject your femininity, but you can't change it. You cannot separate them. So, if you were born a man, you are masculine. If you were born a woman, you are feminine. I then realized that as an athlete, I was able to live out my femininity every time I played my sport or worked out. I was being receptive to pain and suffering, but I was also receptive to my teammates. And in my own way, I was then bearing forth life on my team, through my play, through taking the time to love my teammates, and through my openness and offering my suffering to God.

The very natural difference between masculinity and femininity can be seen in sport. You can see the sexual difference. Let's use basketball as an example. When men play basketball, their play is a little more physical. Men are naturally stronger, and you see a lot more individual play, and men sacrificing their bodies and driving to the hoop and dunking the ball. And when women play, there is more teamwork, more passing, and more plays. The game is said to be "prettier." Since the height of masculinity is sacrifice, men are a little bit more likely to take the ball for themselves and to sacrifice their bodies. Women are naturally more receptive, so there's a lot more teamwork. These different styles of play just reveal something naturally different about us. Not better, not worse; equal but different. Women, we still sacrifice, and men are still receptive, but the height of our call to live out our femininity is in our particular depth of receptivity and bearing forth life. There are many ways as women that we can live out our receptivity in all areas of our lives. We can be good friends, receiving those around us and encouraging them to new life. We can be good employees, students, sisters, mothers, wives, all by being open to others and ultimately open to what God is asking of us.

For years there has been a competition between men and women, or a seeking to nullify the sexual difference. The complementarity shown above is not about one being better than or dominating the other. It is about the beauty of both as they are, and the encouragement of each other in our uniqueness. Ultimately, it is actually the sexual difference that reveals that we are made in the image and likeness of God, "not only through his own humanity, but also through the communion of persons."[2] We as the man, woman, and child reflect the Father, Son and Holy Spirit. It is far too simple an analogy, but God the Father completely loves the Son. The Son receives that love and gives it back to the Father. They say that that love is so palpable, and real, it is creative and "the Holy Spirit proceeds from the Father and the Son" (The Nicene Creed). Similarly, the man has the capacity to love the woman, the woman can receive the love of the man, and return that love. And while God respects our freedom, and we don't perfectly exchange love as He does, nine months later that exchange of love can result in a third, a child. This is why our bodies, as male and female matter. We reflect the Trinity. See diagrams.

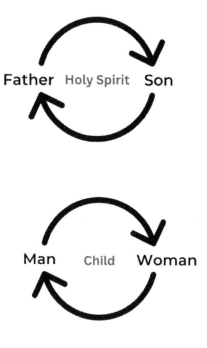

Practice Item

How are you called to live out your femininity? How can you live out your receptivity and your ability to bear forth life on your team? In your sport? In your life? How can you help the men around you live out their call to sacrifice?

4. MENTALLY

A good friend of mine has been the assistant softball coach at a top D1 school for about 25 years. They've won national championships and had a high level of success, so by any estimate she is at the top of the top. What's interesting about the game of softball (or baseball) is that you actually fail 70% of the time, and that's considered good! Players strike out 70% of the time. What this coach points out is that what actually distinguishes the good players from the great players is how they handle failure. To be invited to play at her school means you are a good player. Probably the best from your area. But what elevates all these very good players to become great players, impact players, and leaders is how they deal with the strikeout or the error.

How they rebound from it and come back out. How they handle failure. So how can we as athletes learn to be mentally tough? How can we learn to not close off, which, as we just learned, is opposed to our feminine gift of receptivity? How can we choose to stay open, receptive, and, ultimately, practice a holy mental toughness?

Body Language

The first key to overcoming failure is what we choose to do with our bodies: our body language. How we choose to use or respond with our bodies is a mental decision, a reaction, and a choice. But also, since each of us is a united being, what we do with our bodies actually has a physiological effect on our brains. When you mess up in a game or race, whether it be a missed shot, an error, a trip, or a strikeout, what is the first thing you do? You put your head down and slump your shoulders forward. When your body assumes this posture, there is a physiological reaction that affects your psychology, because a hormonal reaction takes place. Cortisol, which is your stress hormone, goes up, and testosterone (women, we have testosterone too, though in lesser amounts than men), which is your strength hormone, goes down. So literally when you bow your head and close your posture, which is an expression opposed to the openness of our femininity, your body goes up in stress and down in strength. Is that going to help you with the next play? No. However, if you open up, and actually listen to your coach telling you to, "Pick your head up!" there's actually a positive physiological response that happens. Testosterone goes up, cortisol goes down. Strength to engage in the next play, bat up, or leg of the race increases, and the stress and desire to flee decreases.

Now, I'm going to call us out here. I'm calling myself out in this too because I wish somebody had called me out on it years ago. Why else do we actually put our head down? Because we want everybody else to know, that we know, that we messed up. Well, guess what? They already know, and if they didn't, well they do now, thanks to your slumping! It's a matter of pride. It's such a matter of pride. However, we have a choice, and you've probably observed the impact of this choice in games before. If you see somebody mess up, and then they turn around and win the ball back or go into a really hard tackle or encourage the next batter up, that does way more for the team than that player putting their head down and cursing under their breath. I was recently watching a college soccer game with one of the teams I work with, and this girl got the ball stripped from her. She then chases the girl down and cleanly tackles and knocks her down, winning the ball back. It was awesome. I was standing next to that girl's mom on the sidelines. I turned to her mom, and even though before that play they were getting dominated, I said, "that will be the change of tide in this game." And I was right, after that the whole team was fired up and they took total control of the game. They had been inspired by a mentally and physically tough play.

Our bodies speak a language to both our own selves and to others. We also know that as women, we are receptive to one another. So if you react negatively after a mistake, your teammates are going to be more worried about if you are ok, than they are going to be focused on the game. I'm challenging you here. When you make that mental decision not to put your head down, but instead to encourage your teammate, to pump up the next batter by giving them a high five, to chase the puck down, that is going to do more for you and more for your teammates than the alternative. It can literally change the momentum of the game. From this perspective, failure doesn't exist, because if every failure becomes an opportunity to learn, grow, and encourage, we

> Our bodies speak a language to both our own selves and to others.

can use it for the positive. We don't have to be afraid of failure, we can play freely and with excitement to overcome and use all for good.

What's more, is when we react negatively to a bad call or play. If we throw our hands up, scowl at the referee, or make a negative comment, all of those things communicate disrespect for another person as well as distract and derail those around you from the game. If you let a bad call roll off your back, and just keep playing hard, your team is going to follow your body language and lead and do the same. Remember, the referee and the other team, are particular expressions of God. They have eternal worth. You need to treat them that way! Furthermore, God is dwelling in them. We need to treat them with the same reverence we do God, even if that is hard. It is ok to play hard and compete, but not ok to intentionally hurt or mock or yell at others. Also, what is your body communicating when you celebrate after a shot or goal? Is your celebration full of gestures that point to yourself and draw more attention to you, thus distracting or taking away from your teammates? Or are you using the opportunity to encourage those around you, and lift them up?

> **Practice Item**
>
> What is your typical reaction when you mess up in your sport, make a mistake, or a bad call is made? How can you choose to react positively with your body?

Self-Talk

What is the biggest section in any bookstore you go to? Self-help. They say the most important conversation you have in a day is with yourself. And while there is merit to this thought, I actually disagree with it. Self-help brings you only to your own self, your own internal conversation. It's a sign of self-reliance. Self-reliance is actually one of the biggest inhibitors to growth in a truly free and Christian life. Rather, I would argue that the most important conversation that you have in a day is with the Lord. We'll get there in the next chapter. First let's understand a basic psychological principle. Our thoughts become our beliefs, which become our emotions, which become our actions. For example, you miss a shot on goal, or you get scored on, or you trip on the sidewalk with everybody watching. Where does your mind go within a snap of your fingers? "Wow, that was embarrassing. I can't believe I did that. I suck. I shouldn't be on this team. I just want to run away and hide. I don't even deserve to exist." Just like that. Especially for women, we can go to a very, very, very dark place very quickly. We can spiral, and then how does that affect our performance? If you believe that you're worthless, how are

If you believe that you're worthless, how are you going to play well?

you going to play well? Our thoughts become our actions.

We need to learn to combat this negative pattern of thinking, not only for the sake of our performance, but also generally for our mental, emotional, and physical well-being. Two pieces of advice here: first, have a statement; a self-mantra of sorts. Pick something and write it somewhere where you can see it during your game. Root your statement in truth. Not something generic like "You can do this", but something rooted in the truth of who you are: your TRUE identity as a daughter of God and the reality that you are very good and have been created with a purpose. My statement is "I AM ENOUGH." It's helpful to share this statement with someone you can trust because in the heat of the moment, they can help you refocus and not spiral. My best friend knows my statement, so I'll call her, and I'll say something like, "I had the worst day. I shouldn't be running this nonprofit. I suck. What am I doing with my life?" And she'll just say, "I..." and I have to repeat "I", then "am", and then "ENOUGH"! By the time I say "enough", I'm usually pretty calmed down and refocused on the truth.

There's power there. Pick a statement. "I am enough." "I am loved." "I am good." "Jesus is Lord." Whatever it is. Pick something and write it somewhere. I used to tape my wrists when I played soccer and write it on the tape. Then when the ball would go out of bounds, I would quickly glance down, see my statement and it would take me out of my mental spiral.

The mind, through something called neuroplasticity, is like a muscle in the sense that you can train it. It can grow and change and learn new thinking patterns. You have to train your mind out of the dark spiral and into holy mental toughness, rooted in and reclaiming who you are! So, tell a close friend or teammate your statement. They know by your body language if you're struggling in a game, and can remind you, "Hey, you're enough". This is what my doubles partner says to me when we are rowing, and she can see me get frustrated. You'll see that it's more than just a statement. It's actually rooted in truth, and because of that there's actually a spiritual power there.

> ## Practice Item
>
> Pick a statement and share it with a teammate, friend, or fan so they can remind you of it when you need. Make a plan to put it somewhere you can see while you play. Ex: written on your glove, taped around your wrist, held on a sign by a fan.

Beliefs

The second piece of advice I would give you here goes deeper spiritually. It's one for "off the field", because it takes a little bit longer. It has to do with ridding ourselves of the lies, fears, and negative scripts we have running through our minds by combating them with truth and praying through these things repeatedly.

> ## Practice Item:
>
> *Part 1:* When you have some free time, take out a journal or piece of paper, go into prayer, and write down the lies that you believe about yourself. Things like, "I'm not good enough." "I'm ugly." "I'm a failure." "I'm not worthy of love." "I'll always be alone." "If people only knew ____ they'd hate me." "I've done ____ so God can't love me." "I'm afraid of ____." Whatever it is, take time to note what are those negative scripts and accusations that go on in your

mind when you mess up and even in ordinary day-to-day living. Write down those negative statements on one side of a piece of paper, and then on the other side of the piece of paper I want you to write the truth that counteracts the lie or fear. "I am enough." "I am good." "I'm unconditionally loved". "I am beautiful." "I am capable." "I'm never alone." "God is in control of my life".

When those lies come, we really can train ourselves to combat them with truth. From a spiritual perspective, you can even reject and renounce them. These statements are not of God. They are accusations and false lies from the father of lies, Satan. This isn't said to scare you, but rather liberate you. These aren't your fault, and they are the ways that the evil one tries to discourage us. But we don't have to fear because while we struggle with these, Jesus is so much stronger than them. In the name of Jesus, the devil and evil spirits flee because of how powerful He is! So, with every lie you can actually renounce it and take away its power in your life.

Part 2: Renounce the list of lies you wrote down above. As a baptized individual you have authority over yourself to do this. (So, if you're sharing this with and leading another person through this, have them repeat after you and claim this for themselves.) Say the following out loud: "In the name of Jesus Christ, I renounce the lie that _____. I bind it, break ties with it, and send it to the foot of the Cross. I claim the truth that _____ (your corresponding counter statement of truth from the other side of your paper). Thank you, Lord, for setting me free. Bless me Father." There's actual power there. We're taking captive that part of our mind and filling it with good, holy, truthful self-talk: God-talk!

I have worked with several athletes who incorporate this type of prayer into their lives. For example, a girl was feeling nervous and discouraged going into practice after her coach said something negative to her. She renounced what he said and renounced the spirit of anxiety before the next practice, replacing it with the truth that she deserved to be on the team and the spirit of peace. It had a great effect on her play and confidence thereafter. This type of prayer is a tool you can use to play and live with deeper freedom.

Motivation

Underlying the mental side of athletics is our motivation. Why are we doing what we are doing? Is it rooted in love or fear? When we compete, you can really see someone's motivation revealed by its fruits or results. What I mean by this is that you can tell when someone is playing out of fear, or when someone is playing out of freedom because freedom's fruit is confidence.

Every athlete desires to play with confidence. They ultimately desire to play with reckless abandon, totally free to play well and joyfully, knowing that they are loved. This, I think we can all recognize, is no easy feat. Instead, we often are bound by fear. We play in chains, afraid of failure, of messing up, of not starting, of losing, and of what our coach and others will say about us. For most of us, we are somewhere in the middle. We have glimpses of freedom but stay fearful. I'll offer first how to recognize if you are playing in fear, what its unfortunate consequences or fruits are, and their ramifications for your life, your play, and your impact on your team. Then once we have learned "what not to do", we will talk about the ways we can grow and play in deeper freedom.

Fear or Freedom

Let's use off-season training as an example. I would train all summer so that come pre-season I could pass the fitness tests and come in ready to play and compete. But so often when I was training in the summer, I was doing so out of fear. Fear that I wouldn't pass or be good enough, and as a result I fell into what I call the 3 D's: Deception, Debilitation, and Division.

The first fruit of fear is deception. I would deceive myself and tell myself lies. I would tell myself I wasn't going to pass. And it was a defense mechanism, so that if I did not pass the fitness test, I would already be prepared for the disappointment. This is no way to train. It's throwing in the towel before you even start. I think we often train this way. We train but we doubt or try to protect ourselves ahead of time, and this holds us back. We expect the worst, rather than the best! Or we tell ourselves the wrong things. How often when you are out for a run do you just say to yourself, "Don't stop"? When we say this, we are actually deceiving our brains, because our brains focus on the idea of stopping by picturing a big red stop sign! Subconsciously we are interpreting the exact opposite of what we want! We need in this case to say the reverse: "Keep going"!

Second is debilitation. When we are playing, or in this case training, out of fear, then we often find ourselves debilitated. We skip workouts, get discouraged, or worse, we start a workout and don't finish it. You often find this with people who are "perfectionists". They get so overwhelmed by not doing everything perfectly, or the fear that they won't succeed, that they just don't take action. How often do we make an excuse or cut corners in our training? This is because at the root we are afraid to push, to hurt, and in the end to not get the result we want.

Finally, the motivation of fear causes division. When we fear not passing a fitness test, for example, we become self-absorbed. We are so focused on ourselves that we don't recognize the greater picture of the team as a whole. We seek to get ahead, to undercut those around us. We hope that they fail, and we succeed. The result is a rift of division not only in our own hearts towards our teammates, but amongst our teams. This is not the way to get ahead, not truly.

"Our deepest fear is not that we are inadequate. Our deepest fear is that we are powerful beyond measure. It is our light, not our darkness that most frightens us. We ask ourselves, 'Who am I to be brilliant, gorgeous, talented, fabulous?' Actually, who are you not to be? You are a child of God. Your playing small does not serve the world. There is nothing enlightened about shrinking so that other people won't feel insecure around you. We are all meant to shine, as children do. We were born to make manifest the glory of God that is within us. It's not just in some of us; it's in everyone. And as we let our own light shine, we unconsciously give other people permission to do the same. As we are liberated from our own fear, our presence automatically liberates others."

- Marianne Williamson, A Return to Love[3]

How do you recognize if you are training and playing in freedom? We have three points to counteract the three D's above. The first, to counteract deception, is truth. We need to play in the truth of who we are. We learned earlier that our identity is not in our performance, or passing the fitness test, or earning a starting spot. We are daughters of God. When we internalize that our actions don't determine our worth, we learn that the pressure is off. Now some may think that this is an excuse to fail, but I would argue for the opposite. When we know we are loved no matter what, we can run, play, train in total freedom. Love motivates us to push hard and receive the gifts we have been given even deeper.

Second, when we are driven by freedom, we are not debilitated. We take action. We aren't paralyzed by the result, rather we trust the process. We do all the workouts, and we take one step at a time, living in the present moment. We do everything to the best of our ability. We push hard and honor the process. We recognize what we can control, and we learn to surrender the things that we can't control, trusting that ultimately God is in control, and everything will be ok. I once had a priest say to me, "Everything will not be 'ok'. It will be great, because we don't just have an 'ok' God, we have a great one." We need to trust everything will be great!

Finally, playing in freedom is characterized not by division but by unity. We engage in true competition. True competition is not about beating and using others to get ahead, putting others down, or hoping that others don't succeed. True competition is pushing our hardest and encouraging those around us to do the same. Therefore, we both get better in the process. We hope that others come in fit and ready to play too, because that is not only going to make us better players, but the team a better team. Ultimately, it's about true love. It's about loving ourselves and those around us. The opposite of love is use. It's using those around us for our own gain. But true love, as exercised on your team and in your life, is when we will the good of

The opposite of love is use.

those around us, and ourselves. We lay down our lives for others. We unite as a team, sacrifice for one another, encourage one another, and collectively strive for freedom.

So how do we make that journey from fear to freedom? How do we go from deception to truth, from debilitation to action, and from division to unity? First, let's rid ourselves of the expectations. Rid yourself of the expectations and pressures you put on yourself to be perfect. Rid yourself of the expectations your parents put on you, your coaches, and your teammates. Write down and renounce all of these like we learned in the practice item above. Remember and know that you are loved as you are. No matter whether you pass the fitness tests and start or have to do extra fitness and sit the bench, you are loved the same. Root yourself in your identity as God's daughter and play in the freedom only He can promise us through His grace, love, mercy, and salvation. Second, compete truly. Compete in a way that calls those around you higher, not stepping on them or wishing for their demise or injury in hopes of getting ahead. You should crave good competition with those that will push you and make you better, and you them! This is living fully and embracing your talents that God gave you to be the best you can be.

Finally, play differently. Others should look at how you play and train, how you interact with others, and how you speak, and know you are a Christian without you ever telling them. Sharing your faith is needed, don't get me wrong, but how we act is also a witness. You should be the hardest working person on your team. You should be the kindest, most patient, most grateful, and most humble person on your team. If you truly realize your core identity, and the gifts and opportunities you have been given, then everything you do is an act of honoring God. You honor Him with your talent by pushing as hard as you can and never cutting corners, doing everything asked of you (and more) with joy, and playing in freedom. You honor Him by honoring those around you: your teammates and your competition. Finally, may everything you say honor God. We need to be positive, pure, and true in our language. This journey takes practice, but the result is freedom and a holy mental toughness.

Practice Item

Reflect on: Do I play, train, and compete in fear or in freedom? How can I make that journey from fear to freedom? How can I, in all I do, honor the Lord better?

5. SPIRITUALLY

I think athletes have an amazing disposition to a robust spiritual life. We already value the discipline of putting in daily training for something. We know that we have to practice and train in order to grow and meet our competition goals. Well, it's the same with our relationship with the Lord. Our spiritual life takes practice. It takes consistency in order to grow. And while in many ways, spiritual growth is not as tangible as physical growth, greater depth and intimacy with God comes from giving him the time to speak to us. While prayer is mostly for our own needs, the Lord desires our love as well. We have already seen, and will continue to see, how our faith can and should pervade all areas of our lives.

Building a Relationship

If you and I had never met, and I was to call you on the phone and say "Hey, how are you?" would you respond with honesty? With telling me how you actually were and being vulnerable and telling me your deepest secrets? No! You would say, "Um, who is this? And what do you want?!" Well let's say you and I got to know each other over time. We became close friends and were able to entrust each other with different things. Then one day, I called you on the phone and again said, "Hey, how are you?" First, you would recognize my voice right away, and second, you'd be a lot more open with me. Well just like any relationship, our relationship with God takes both time and consistency. One of the most common questions I hear is, "How do I know God's voice?" Well, just like when I called you in that second instance, God's voice becomes quite distinct to us after we have spent considerable time with Him. If you're not praying, the best thing you can do is spend 10 minutes a day talking to God. Remain consistent, and as you would get to know a friend, you'll get to know Him. Read Scripture, because it is God's playbook, of sorts. It is "God-breathed" and Holy-Spirit-inspired. You can pray certain prayers, pray for others, attend Mass or services and you can just chat with him like you would a friend. If you are Catholic, you have access to the Sacraments as a way to obtain grace daily from God to grow closer to Him. I often think of Confession as an ice bath for your soul! And the Eucharist is the most prized and intimate gift you can receive from God – His very self, united with you as your spiritual nourishment. You may even want to consider getting a spiritual director or spiritual mentor, which is a priest, religious, or lay person trained in helping guide or "coach" you in your spiritual life.

Beyond your personal "get to know God time", everything in your day can become an interaction with God. When we know God loves us, and has given us everything we have, we come to see him everywhere. We see and experience His presence everywhere. We see Him in the beautiful sunrise in the morning, knowing He is showing off for us. We see Him in the bluebird that flies by and makes us smile, knowing He had us in mind when He created the bluebird. He even knew that we would see it at that exact moment, and it would make us happy. We even begin to see Him in the person that cuts us off in traffic. Not only is it a chance to grow in the virtue of patience and temperance, fighting the urge for road rage, but also a chance to respond with charity and pray for someone (that driver) whom maybe no one else would pray for that day.

Practice Item

Make a prayer game plan. When and how are you going to spend time getting to know God? (Maybe start by reading a chapter of the Gospel of John per day or listen to a few minutes of a Catholic or Christian Podcast and reflect on it.)

Active Faith

When it comes to your sport, realizing that your athletic ability is an endowed gift from God allows you to really give that gift back to the Lord and "pray always" while competing. Like I said earlier, people should know that you're a Christian or a Catholic by how hard you play on the field. Some people have a disposition where they think, "If I know I'm a daughter of God, and my worth isn't based on what I do, then it doesn't matter how hard I try in practice. I'm still loved the same." While this is true, I'd say it completely misses the point of daughterhood. I would say it's the opposite. Rather we should say, "I know how good I am because of what God has done for me, and I know that my athletic talent is a gift from Him, and so you better believe that I'm going to be the hardest worker on my team, that I'm never going to cut corners, that I'm going to be an example because this is all a gift." The fact that you get to do your sport is a gift and what you do with that gift is how you show gratitude to God for giving it to you. It's a gift for us, but the cool thing is, we can pay that gift forward and offer that gift back.

It's something called offering up. You've probably heard this your whole life. You stub your toe, and your grandmother's like, "Offer it up." Right? Well, what's really cool is through our faith, we know that suffering is redemptive. We know that in God's crazy plan, He allows us to pray for other people, and He actually listens. Similarly, we can offer our pain and our suffering up as a prayer, and it's not just some flippant comment, "Oh, I'm offering it up." St. Paul says in Colossians 1: 24 "I am now rejoicing in my sufferings for your sake, and in my flesh, I am completing what is lacking in Christ's afflictions for the sake of his body, that is, the church." (NRSV). What St. Paul is not saying is that Christ's affliction, and death was not enough to save humanity. It was. However, we in our afflictions can unite with Christ and offer it for "His Church", i.e., those in our lives who need prayers. When Jesus died on the Cross, He offered His body and His soul. He sweat blood in the Garden of Gethsemane, He experienced excruciating pain when He was flogged and crowned with thorns. He was dehydrated and thirsty. His muscles cramped and gave out as He carried His Cross. He couldn't breathe when He was nailed to it. Does that sound familiar? In a small, small, small way, every time we workout, practice, race or play we experience these similar sufferings. Therefore, we can literally take that suffering, unite it with Christ's and offer it up for somebody else.

In college, before every practice, as I was jogging over to the field, I would bless myself and say, "Lord, I offer this practice for _____." For games, I would write the intention I was offering the game up for on my wrist tape, on the opposite side as my positive mental statement. Then when the ball went out of bounds, or I had a moment to pause, I would look down and remember who I was playing and suffering for. Tuesdays were conditioning days. After practice we would run sprints. I used to get on the line with the intent of offering my sprints for my teammates. For example, say we were going to do ten 120-meter sprints. I'd say all right, "this first sprint is for Savannah, next to me. Lord, I know she doesn't know you and wants to. I know she's struggling right now in her faith life so please bless her." I'd run that sprint as hard as I could for her. Next, Calie. "I know what Calie did on Saturday night, Lord, and I know she's hurting, and I know she's longing. This is for her." Next Anne. "Anne's mom's really sick right now, Lord, please bless both Anne and her mom." When I lifted weights, I would whisper different girls' names under my breath every rep. It became about more than just me.

This can include your injury as well. Injuries are a suffering. We have such an opportunity to offer up our sufferings for those around us. After college, I spent some time as a missionary, working as a spiritual coach for athletes on a D1 college campus. One of the athletes that I was getting to know had to have her second labral tear in her hip repaired the year after winning a national championship. This was devastating to her, as she had already had the other operated on just a year before. Around the time her hip began bothering her, mine did too. Probably from years of overuse in soccer, but God used the timing perfectly. We ended up having right labral hip repair surgery just 30 days apart. And we journeyed through rehab together. I would text her things like, "I'm offering up my leg lifts for you today", and after a while, she started to do the same for me. This built trust and I offered my whole surgery and recovery so that she would come to know God deeper and have a personal relationship with Christ and know that she was loved. One day in mass, amidst the

> We have such an opportunity to offer up our sufferings for those around us.

sorrow of dealing with her injury, she felt God say those very words to her and she knew that she was loved. Her life changed trajectory after that. She is a beautiful and radiant woman of faith now. While that offering was a clear calling from the Lord for me, we never know the effects we can have on others by offering our suffering for them.

I'd like to note, we should always pray and ask God to heal us when we get injured. I have seen ACLs miraculously repaired through prayer. And whether it be through a miracle, the hands of a surgeon, the body's natural healing ability, or one day in Heaven when our bodies are glorified, God promises healing. So, pray for healing, and until it comes, offer up your sufferings.

Practice Item

Who are you going to offer your miles, sprints, weight reps, shots taken, or rehab for? Who are you going to offer your practice or game or injury up for? Where can you write this intention for your next game? (wrist tape, glove, stick, etc.)

Receptive Faith

We have spent a lot of time talking about the practical ways in which we can grow in our faith lives. Our prayer becomes the undercurrent of all we do, from our practicing and play, to our interactions with our teammate and others, to our mental toughness. There is another facet of the faith life that I want to introduce, and that is intimate union with God. This type of prayer and faith is different because it is not about "doing", it's about receiving. As athletes, we are doers, and so the thought of receptive prayer can be hard to wrap our minds about. Receptive prayer is not a passive process. Rather, it requires an active receptivity. I would liken it to surfing. In surfing, you have to work hard to paddle out into the ocean past the breaking point of the waves. This is an arduous task, requiring you to paddle against the current and dive over and under waves. But after all this hard work, once you get past the point where the wave breaks, you wait. But it's not a passive waiting. You have to wait with anticipation and readiness to receive a wave at any moment. This is where the beauty of receptivity is seen. The surfer has to wait for the perfect wave to come.

Receptive prayer, likewise, takes some work to get into the position to receive God. We have to set aside a set time and space to pray in. This can be hard, and many things can distract us or convince us that making this consistent prayer time isn't worth it or is too hard. But God is within you. He is waiting for you to close your eyes, go into prayer, and begin to look for him in your heart. For us to meet him there, it is not a matter of doing, but of receiving. It requires going before God in prayer and in silence (which they say is God's favorite language) and finding Christ. Surrender and receptivity are a lifelong journey, a daily act. He wants to interact with you, be with you, listen to you, teach you, hug you, hold you, cry with you, reassure you, have a cup of coffee with you, go on a run with you. It may sound funny, but many times in prayer, Jesus and I sit down for a cup of coffee, as friends would, and talk. Other times, He holds a punching bag for me to healthily let out my frustrations and give them to Him. Still others He is a coxswain in my boat telling me to just keep rowing, He will steer me where we need to go. And this is not just reserved for Christ. Who is the Holy Spirit to you? What about God the Father? What about Mary, His Mother? Your favorite saint? Prayer is both intimate and fun in this way. There is always more depth. You may still feel uncertain about this. Maybe you have tried this type of prayer and feel like you don't know what you are doing… good! I have felt this sentiment many times. I also can show up to prayer and feel like I don't know what to do or how to do it. This is not about performing or being perfect. St. Paul says in Romans 16:18, "We do not know how to pray as we ought." That was St. Paul, the greatest evangelist of all time and even he didn't feel like He knew how to pray adequately. The best we can do is create a time and quiet sacred space for God to enter in. Regularity and consistency are key here. Once you do those things, then it is time for you to receive.

Practice Item

For the next week, plan how to spend 15 minutes in silent receptive prayer every day.

Preparing for Prayer

Let's go deeper. Maybe it is the active spirit I have, the go-getter mentality, but learning to receive has been one of the hardest things for me to learn in prayer, even though as a woman I am built for it, and as the Bride, the Church, we are all called to it in relation to Christ. Along the way, some wise priests have shared with me, both the "to-do's" of this intimate spousal prayer, but also the "don't-do's".

These are things that I have put in place, trying to orient my prayer time. I share them with you in order to hope you too learn to receive.

First, we need to defend our prayer, however. Defend this space you have created. As you pray, make note of your primary, secondary, and tertiary distractions. What makes your mind wander or interrupts you. Is it your phone? To do list? Those you love? Your neighbor's music? Your family? These are important things to make a plan against. For example, plan to not take your phone to prayer. To get up earlier when you can be alone to pray. To go to a chapel. To shut the door to your room. To redirect your wandering thoughts back to the face of Christ. These are the waves of distraction we must recognize and fight against. This is the part you can make a game plan for. The rest is up to God.

Practice Item:

Identify your 3 biggest distractions in prayer and make a game plan of how to avoid these distractions.

Entering Into Prayer

As you approach this time of intimate prayer – time that you have already learned now to protect - don't have an agenda. This prayer is not like that. We are not looking at it to "get anything out of it", or as an item to check off the list, or as another task to complete. Sometimes I approach prayer wondering, even nervous, as to what is going to happen in it. First of all, it's completely normal for us, as broken human beings, to be afraid of God. It's not necessary, because He is utter love, and yet in our brokenness we fear Him. We should not be afraid of His love and intimacy. It's wild. When I fret about prayer, it's because I am unsettled, or I'm putting parameters on God, or I'm projecting what I think prayer should be or look like. Again, receptive prayer isn't for me to lead. It's for Him to lead. And He is always much more than we can ever comprehend, so that this type of prayer will never cease to be growing and deepening. Put yourself in an open posture that allows you to be surprised by God, who will always be one step ahead of you.

Look at Him. Look Christ in the eyes or look upon the Father. When we look at Him, whether that be through how we picture Him in our depths, through His spoken word to us in scripture, or through sacred art or an icon, we are forced to come out of ourselves. We are helped to stop navel gazing at our own pain and hurts, anxieties, and fears. **God is Primary.** All of our worries, anxieties, fears, intentions, will melt away. They don't matter in the presence of God because God IS the answer to all of them. The things that weigh us down, He hears, sees, and takes. I also often picture myself unloading all my burdens to Mary, so that I can enter deeper into unburdened prayer. I trust that she takes all of my intentions to her Son. The worries melt away, and our longing for God begins to grow.

Many of us are spectators at prayer. We are spectators at a game, rather than playing in it. We do our intercessions, pray our rosary, even spend quiet time with the Lord, but we don't jump in. It's like watching the ocean from the shore and admiring it, verses jumping full into it and experiencing its power, depths, and freshness. Let go and jump in. It will be particular to your heart, and beyond what you imagine. Let God lead. Sometimes He will be silent and sometimes He will talk nonstop. Sometimes you will feel His presence and sometimes you will just know He is there. When you come before Him with a desire to be with Him, just to be, it delights Him greatly, and that is enough. That type of prayer, that relationship, is all we need to sustain us. It meets and satisfies our deepest longings and desires. This is what we were created for.

Practice Item

When you enter into your 15 minutes of prayer, turn off all distractions and just be with Him, even when it's uncomfortable. Go inside your heart and find Christ. Let Him lead you. Where is He? What is He doing? What does He look like? What does He say to you? After your 15 minutes is up, write down some of these things in a journal.

Your Mission

Flowing from our prayer is the capacity to enter into what God desires us to do for Him and for others. Your sport is about more than just you. It's your mission. One day, after I'd had a deep encounter with the Lord and was really trying to live my faith, I was in this practice. My specialty as a soccer player was heading the ball. I mean I'm six feet tall, so that kind of worked well. Anyway, I was in the middle of this heading drill, and essentially what would happen is somebody would cross the ball, and I would have to jump and head or volley it on goal. Specialty. Love this. I'd dive, I'd fly, I'd jump over people. It was great. This particular day, I kid you not, I could not score a goal for the life of me. I hit the post three times. I hit the crossbar twice. I must have had at least 15 attempts missing, and I was getting more and more angry. I'd never done this before, and at our level, you didn't do this, but I literally stepped off the field in the middle of the drill. When I had a moment, I uttered this prayer/cry/yell in my heart. I just said, "God, I'm done. This isn't fun anymore." And what I meant by that is, yes, I was way over the heading drill, but this was my junior year, and as I was going into my senior year, I really hadn't seen the field much. It had taken about three years for my knee to recover, and while I was resolved to not be a quitter and finish up my senior year, I was not going to take my available red-shirt fifth year. I was done. I thought, "I'm out of here. This has been a complete failure."

What I heard Him say in that moment was, "Samantha, that's because it's not about you." It was like a God sucker-punch. He'll do that to us. He said, "It's not about you." What I realized in that moment is that I was still playing for my own expectations. I wanted to be the one to come back from this career ending injury, to become the star again. He revealed to me that if I left, who was going to reach my teammates? I was the only practicing Christian on my team. Who was going to reach them? I was put on that team at that time for a particular reason and that was to love my teammates. Sometimes that was picking them up at 2:00AM. Sometimes that was inviting them to Bible study and Mass. It was particular to each girl's needs. And you know what? I finally played with freedom and returned to my true love for the game, and because of that became an impact player both on and off the field. I ended up taking a fifth year, becoming captain, and starting, but I'm most proud of looking back on the relationships built with my teammates those last two years. The 12 girls that would pray with me before games, they became my mission. Our gifts become how we love the world. We each have a task as unique as we are, that only we can fulfill. That may be asking your teammates how you can pray for them. That may be, even though you're not starting, being an impact player from the bench and learning to support and cheer for those on the field. That may be being the leading scorer and using your platform to help and lead others. Whatever it is, you have an important role and task only you can do, and

> We each have a task as unique as we are, that only we can fulfill.

when done with love and humility, is a gift to the Lord and to others.

Practice Item

Reflect on your own personal gifts from a physical perspective, a mental perspective, a spiritual perspective, then ask the question, "God, how are you calling me to love more?" "What is my task right now?" "Where have you uniquely placed me at this moment in time to reach those around me?" Listen to what he has to say and enter into your mission!

6. YOU ARE NOT ALONE

Who's in your corner? As athletes we are used to being a part of a team. We are used to growing together, being pushed together, competing together. The same is true with becoming a FIERCE athlete. Reading this book, doing the practice items, is the beginning of a journey. In order to continue this new way of playing your sport and living your life, I want to encourage you to find a team.

I want to be sensitive to the fact that some of you reading this book may have a great support system of sport and faith. Whether that be a faith-filled family member, friend, mentor, or teammate. If this is the case, I want you to share this book with them, and lean into their support in these areas.

For some of you, someone who you know is faithful and handed you this book. If you were initially skeptical, I'm glad you decided to give it a read. First of all, thank you for having the courage to get this far. There may have been some very new things in here. Continue to dig deeper.

Finally, some of you may be like I was. You may have read this and looked around at your team and realized you are seemingly the only one who wants to live a Christian life. First, there is always room for invitation to others. A book like this is a non-threatening way to reach someone. Give it to them. Start a book study or small group on your team or with your friends. You can be in their corner. But make sure you find a group of people, even outside your sport or here at FIERCE Athlete, to support you on your mission.

Ultimately though, I hope you realize you have a perfect spiritual support team. You have all the angels and saints in heaven rooting for you, praying for you. We can look to those who have gone before us for inspiration and courage. Saints like St. Joan of Arc, St. Philomena, Mother Teresa, and St. John Paul II are prime examples of lives lived courageously. Ultimately there is no place that Christ has not been, no life he cannot fill with courage. He is with you always.

CONCLUSION

Jesus was the ultimate athlete. What He went through in His Passion and Death, none of us could ever endure. He left us a model: The Gospel of Suffering. Christ suffered for you and me in order to take on the punishment that was owed to us. He who knew no sin, took on sin, endured brutal torture and death, and rose again from the dead. He did all of this, with you in mind. He did it for you, and also to show you "that nothing again would be casual or small", (from a favorite poem of John Cardinal O'Connor)[4]. He has shown us that we are all called to BE FIERCE; physically, mentally, and spiritually. We are called to take this to all arenas of our lives, and to use our gifts and talents to share the joy of faith and living life to the full with others.

Consider yourself now part of the FIERCE Athlete family. God Bless you.

ENDNOTES

1. https://www.dove.com/us/en/stories/about-dove/our-research.html

2. John Paul II. 20011. Man and Woman He Created Them: A Theology of the Body. Boston, MA: Pauline Books and Media.

3. Williamson, Marianne. 1996. A Return to Love. New York, NY: HarperCollins.

4. *I Sing of a Maiden*, by Rev. John Duffy, C.S.S.R.

ABOUT FIERCE ATHLETE

FIERCE Athlete exists in order to promote true identity and femininity in female athletics based on the teachings of the Catholic Church. It desires to foster and equip an army of fierce, integrated, current and former female athletes who will positively impact the culture of sport. For more information, resources, and to get involved please visit www.fierce.org.

BE FIERCE

ABOUT THE AUTHOR

Samantha Kelley is an international presenter, author, and speaker. She is the Founder and current President of FIERCE Athlete Inc. She was a 9x state champion in high school between soccer, ice hockey and track. She played Division I Soccer at UConn and is currently involved in competitive rowing, pickleball, and triathlons. She holds a Masters in Catholic Psychology, Certification in Strength & Conditioning and has extensively studied the Theology of the Body. Through FIERCE she desires to reach female athletes, coaches, and parents across the world and change the culture of female athletics. She currently resides in Pennsylvania with her golden retriever Birdie.

Made in the USA
Middletown, DE
04 September 2024

59742714R00062